THE GOD GIRL'S GUIDE TO COLLEGE LIFE

THE GOD GIRL'S GUIDE TO COLLEGE LIFE

MYA KAY

Girls Anthem, LLC.

ISBN: 978-0-578-39542-5

First paperback edition April 2022

Edited by Girls Anthem, LLC.
Cover Art (Girl): karolinal (depositphotos.com)
Cover Art Layout by Mya Kay

Printed in the USA

Girls Anthem, LLC.
6595 Roswell Road
Suite G2513
Atlanta, GA. 30328

www.girlsanthem.biz
www.writermya.com

Contents

FRESHMAN YEAR

I

What's the Real Focus?

Dear God,

I know that You have big plans for me that I have yet to understand. Growing up in church I was always taught the importance of remaining pure, not getting pregnant out of wedlock and to make sure I prepare to be somebody's wife. If I'm honest, I know that's not Your complete focus. They are important, but they aren't the most important. Before I'm a wife, I am your daughter and I have gifts and talents that I have yet to discover. Lord, I want to ask You what my focus should be. Help me to see what You see in me. I may not have all the answers and pieces now, but I want to know that I'm focusing on what You would have me to. Even in staying pure, I need a solid plan that isn't one shoved down my throat but speaks to my journey alone. Reveal to me more of who You are, more of who You want me to be and how to walk this thing out. So, when I ask what's the focus, I want Your will for my life and not my church family's or my parents. You had a design for my life before I was in my mother's womb, so you know every step I will take, even when I misstep. So, with purity, purpose and everything in between, show me who I'm called to be without the pressure. I trust Your plan for my life to unfold in Your timing.

In Jesus name, Amen.

<u>*Reality Check*</u>

Listen, when I was growing up in church, especially during my middle school years, they shoved purity down our throats. All I remember hearing is, "no boyfriend and girlfriend in the church", "no sex before marriage" and "we're preparing you to be a wife". If one of my homegirls went to her prom with a little of her navel showing, she certainly was sinning. "How could you let the world see your birth line?" Somehow, I knew that couldn't be all God was concerned about. I named this first chapter "What's the Real Focus?" because while purity is very important to God, so are the other parts of our lives. I truly believe that because we were told not to have sex so much, we were more inclined to want to try it — and I did. But it wasn't because it was forbidden. I was touched at four-years-old by a girl who was twelve. Had someone sat down and asked me why I decided to lose my virginity, they would know that touching myself was no longer satisfying to me. What I had been exposed to at four had trickled into my childhood with a force that could only be described as demonic oppression. The real focus for God is our wholeness. He knows that many of us were born into unfair circumstances or situations that we didn't ask for. It wasn't until I was thirty-five, almost three years ago, that I received complete deliverance in this area. Why? Because I had to re-program my mind to get out of this funk that because I was no longer a virgin and still struggled with masturbation that God couldn't use me in life. Listen — I know this first chapter is hitting you hard, but I don't believe in sugar coating anything. In fact, many of my friends that I grew up with are still going through therapy because the church sugarcoated things for far too long. This isn't just a devotional to get you through the hard times during your college life. It's meant to help you walk in the freedom God has already ordained for you. Freedom isn't found in "when I graduate, get my dream job and get married". God's freedom is for you right now and He wants you to tap into it before you succumb to the world's lies that freedom is found in living your best life. There is no best life without God. Heal from your childhood trauma and let God use it for His glory. That's the real focus.

Scripture Meditation:

Mark 5:27-29
She had heard about Jesus, so she came up behind him through the crowd and touched his robe. For she thought to herself, "If I can just touch his robe, I will be healed." Immediately the bleeding stopped, and she could feel in her body that she had been healed of her terrible condition.

Matthew 6:33
Seek the Kingdom of God above all else, and live righteously, and he will give you everything you need.

Psalm 34:17-19
The Lord hears his people when they call to him for help. He rescues them from all their troubles. The Lord is close to the brokenhearted; he rescues those whose spirits are crushed. The righteous person faces many troubles, but the Lord comes to the rescue each time.

Reflection Questions

1. What do you feel God is saying to you in this chapter?

____

____

____

____

2. Do you believe that in pursuing God for yourself, you're focusing on something that was passed down from your parents versus focusing on what God may want you to focus on? If so, what are you focusing on?

____

____

____

____

3. Now that you know God is for your healing and wholeness more than anything, what areas will you start to work on in your own life?

____

____

____

____

4. How can you change your daily quiet time to reach that goal?

____

____

____

____

2

Chosen Path

Dear God,

I know that there's a specific career choice that You have in mind for me. I don't want to get caught up in what my parents feel I should study or even what I think is a safe career choice. You don't want me to live in fear of the economy or what careers may or may not be poppin' ten years from now. You want me to trust that no matter what path You choose for me, that You'll bring me to a place of abundance and overflow. Yes, there will be hard times and obstacles along the way, but if it's the path You choose for me, I will prosper in the ways You want me to prosper. Help me not choose a path based on a salary or on popularity but help me to tap into Your presence daily to uncover my gifts and talents. I want to partner with You to use those gifts for Your glory. This could mean me switching majors even now, but I trust You. This could even mean me taking some time off to re-group and You having me go in a completely different direction. Help me to be still to hear Your still, small voice in the midst of my own thoughts and my parent's wishes. I don't want to let them down, but I have to live for You. They deposited great things into my life, and I will always value that, but I live to please You. Even if my parents didn't give me every-thing that I feel I needed, I thank You that they did their best and You will guide me along the path for my life. Show me that chosen path, Lord. Help me not to get frustrated when there's no clear and cut answer. Help me to lean in and trust that You are ordering my steps, one at a time. I trust You.

In Jesus name, Amen.

<u>Reality Check</u>

I knew that being a doctor was going to be my path. I had chosen it for myself based off what people encouraged me to do when I was a child. I would hear "you're going to be a doctor or a lawyer" so much growing up that I literally entered Community College of Philadelphia with the idea that I would be studying Nursing. Then, when I got to Temple University, I switched to Pre-Med. And guess what? I struggled immensely. I was getting C's in classes that I needed at least a B in. Yet, I still didn't see the signs. I could do this. I had to become a doctor. Why? Because it made sense. I had a love for writing from early childhood, but I didn't want to be a struggling artist. I didn't know anyone in my family or neighborhood that was a doctor or a lawyer. But I knew singers who hadn't made it, writers who were struggling and rappers who fell to their demise with one wrong move. Isn't it crazy how we can see more bad examples in the thing we love to do than good ones? I also remembered hearing "You can't work in Hollywood or go to college in New York. Those are sin dens." No, I'm serious. I had heard that from a pastor and from people who knew I had a creative bug. Again, it goes back to what's the real focus if you're only giving me rules to follow, but no roadmap on how to follow them or to at least seek God's face to make sure this applies to me. So, you can imagine my surprise when God told me to drop my pre-med major and focus on journalism full-time (I was a double major). I couldn't believe it. I mean, how could I write for a secular magazine (Essence magazine)? Wouldn't that be displeasing to God? I'm so glad that even while I didn't fully understand, I followed God's leading and did what He asked. Today, I'm a fourteen-time author (fifteen if you count this book) and I've had great success and exposure in the publishing and journalism industries. Doors opened for me that I never would've imagined. I even had the opportunity to be the assistant to the founder of the NAACP Image Awards in 2019, which gave me front row access to people that could help me take my writing career further. What I wished I had when I was growing up in church was a book like this and others like it that taught me how to pray God's will over my life. I would've saved a year in college instead of being a two-time senior (but I have no regrets – those years were so dope). Here's the key thing to keep in mind: No matter what you do, your greatest job will be to make disciples for Christ. So, whether you're in the boardroom or the operating room, we all have the same purpose – creating disciples for Christ and taking His word to the nations. If you keep that at the center of your prayers, God will give you a career and path that will blow your mind.

<u>Scripture Meditation:</u>

Matthew 28:19
Therefore, go and make disciples of all the nations, baptizing them in the name of the Father and the Son and the Holy Spirit.

Matthew 7:21
"Not everyone who calls out to me, 'Lord! Lord!' will enter the

Kingdom of Heaven. Only those who actually do the will of my Father in heaven will enter.

Psalm 32:8

The Lord says, "I will guide you along the best pathway for your life. I will advise you and watch over you."

Isaiah 30:21

Your own ears will hear him. Right behind you a voice will say, "This is the way you should go," whether to the right or to the left.

Reflection Questions

1. What do you feel God is saying to you in this chapter?

____

____

____

____

2. Are you studying something right now that you don't really have a desire for? Explain whether the answer is 'yes' or 'no'.

____

____

____

____

3. List some ways that you feel you have been forced to go a certain way or pursue a certain path.

____

____

____

____

4. Are you willing to give up your chosen path for God's? Explain.

____

____

____

____

3

No Institution

Dear God,

I feel stuck. If I'm honest, I think I know what You want me to do, but I'm afraid to do it. I've enrolled in some classes, but I feel this tugging on my heart to not go to college. It feels weird because everyone says that getting a degree is the best thing to do. Where I'm from, kids like me don't get many options and I don't want to lose this opportunity, but I don't think this is what You want me to do with my life. I want to make the best decision that pleases You and sets me up for success. Not worldly success, but the success You want me to have. I pray that You would guide this decision. I pray You give me a plan that makes sense for my journey and not someone else's. I refuse to let my parents or loved ones live their dreams through me. While I don't fully know what You're calling me to do, I do know that You're telling me not to go to college. I want to obey You and trust that as I take one step, You'll release my next instruction. Give me the courage to obey You in the midst of this confusion. I don't want to waste time and money on a path that isn't for me and I don't want to assume that college is the only way You can get me to my destination. Take the lead God and pull me in the direction You want me to go. No matter how hard it may be, I trust You to place my feet on solid ground. You will never forsake the righteous and You won't let me fall down. I'd rather fail with You than succeed without You. Give me the words to say to let my parents know the decision I'm about to make. Even if they don't understand, help me to explain in love and still walk away with the full intention to obey You. If I'm honest, I wanted to go to college with my friends and experience all the things that make college fun, but no experience without Your covering is worth it. I surrender to You today.

In Jesus name, Amen.

Reality Check

This one is big. Last year, I met a young lady who I interviewed on my podcast. I knew she was an actress, but I didn't know her full story. I was surprised to hear her say that she didn't go to college. She was nineteen at the time (you can listen to her interview on my podcast, *The Goal Files, Season 3, Episode 1*). I was also impressed with her conviction to follow God over man. She had questioned her decision of course, because all her friends were off to college after graduation, yet she was home focusing on her dream of becoming a full-time actress. Then, Covid hit and she realized that God knew what He was doing all along. Most times, God will tell you to do something and you'll have to obey without knowing why. That's not to say that because of Covid, people had horrible experiences in college, but she knew that God had protected her from having a rough experience in her first year. He was also protecting her dreams. Can you trust God to provide education for you without the institution?

Can you trust Him to lead you along the path that's best for you, even if that means no college? I'm sure it was hard for her to sit back and watch her friends move on with their lives and yet, she has yet to get that big leading role she is believing God for. I have a similar story. I thought trying to go back to school for nursing after I had graduated from graduate school was a good idea. I kept praying that God would open a door, but He didn't. I was trying to escape the nightmare of living my dreams (I was struggling financially, and my books weren't selling) and I was willing to disobey God just to have some relief. But I realized that it was better to struggle temporarily than to struggle permanently because I was out of God's will. Psalm 91 is one of my favorite passages of scripture. The first verse says that "He who dwells in the secret place of the Most High shall abide under the shadow of the Almighty". We can only abide under His shadow when we're where He is. A shadow is used to describe proximity to something. You want to be where God is no matter what the cost. Trust me, it'll be worth it in the end.

Scripture Meditation:

1 Samuel 15:22
But Samuel replied, "What is more pleasing to the Lord: your burnt offerings and sacrifices or your obedience to his voice? Listen! Obedience is better than sacrifice, and submission is better than offering the fat of rams."

Deuteronomy 11:8
"Therefore, be careful to obey every command I am giving you today, so you may have strength to go in and take over the land you are about to enter.

Jeremiah 29:11

For I know the plans I have for you," says the Lord. "They are plans for good and not for disaster, to give you a future and a hope.

Reflection Questions

1. What do you feel God is saying to you in this chapter?

____

____

____

____

2. Do you feel that you can pursue what God has placed on your heart without college? Please note: Do not drop out of college. Very few people are called to make this decision, but it's worth talking to God about.

____

____

____

____

3. Find two examples of Christians who didn't go to college (or didn't finish) but have successful lives. Write three things you learned from them.

____

____

____

____

4. How can you balance being in college with pursuing all that God has placed in your heart? For example, I was studying journalism, but also writing on the side.

____

____

____

____

4

Identity Crisis

Dear God,

I feel like I'm drowning in my identity. I have the world telling me one thing and I have Your word telling me something different. It's hard trying to stay grounded in who You've called me to be when I feel so lost and confused. If I'm honest, it seems like the world has more fun. It seems like they are doing what they want, yet they aren't suffering. I know that You've called me to be set apart so that I can be an honorable vessel for Your use. I feel like the more I cling to You, the more I lose. Help me to get through this identity crisis by helping me to remember that who I am has nothing to do with what I am called to do. I am Your daughter first. I am an heir of Christ and I'm seated in heavenly places with Christ. I am not my accomplishments or my major. I pray that You help these racing thoughts to calm down whenever I try to draw closer to You and the enemy tries to tell me that You don't love me or that You don't care about me. I know You see me, and You care about every detail of my life. Lord, sometimes, I feel like I'm losing more of myself, but I know that's just You shaping me into who You've called me to be. Help me to lean into that and not what I'm losing in the process of becoming more like You. This season has brought me to my knees like never before and I know that this was Your intention. In this crushing, You're not trying to hurt me. You know who I'll be five years from now and in order for me to become that I have to step outside of my comfort zone and let You shape my identity. It may scare me, and it may make me feel like the person You're calling me to be is way bigger than me, but if You're calling me to her, then You placed something inside of me that can become her. Help me to trust You and release the grip that I have on the world. Free me from the grip it has on me.

In Jesus name, Amen.

Reality Check

One of the reasons this prayer probably hit your spirit so hard while you were reading it is because my life story is weaved through-out this prayer. This was me – fighting to maintain my identity in a society that told me I needed to adjust to it in order to survive. I got saved when I was nine on April 24th, 1994. I could feel God molding me then, but I fought hard against it. For some reason, the harder I fought, the more God fought for me. He knew the plans He had for me, yet I was telling God that He didn't know what He was doing, especially as I got older. I didn't want Him to be right. If I'm honest, I didn't want God to choose me. What I didn't realize is that while I may not have wanted Him to choose me, that didn't mean I needed to follow the ways of the world. College is where so many young women lose more of themselves trying to chase after friends and a world that could care less about them. Your friends can't tell you who you are. Your parents can't even tell you who you are. Only

God knows your real identity. This is why staying connected to Him early on in college is so important. Cling to your Savior. There will be so many opportunities to disconnect from God and to do things your way or the world's way. The challenge is that once you start walking in disobedience, the enemy will continue to lure you to do things his way. I've seen friends spiral out of control all because they were trying to fit into spaces and places that God didn't call them to. I have adult friends still doing this, so don't think it stops when you graduate from college. This is why being anchored in who God called you to be early on in life will benefit you later down the line. You don't want to be fifty still telling God 'no'. Surrender now so He can give you your true identity. Lastly, don't let this world lie to you and tell you that you can be whatever and whoever you choose. God created male and female and that's it. You will be persecuted for not following the world's standards and that's okay. Jesus and His followers were persecuted. God is never in the midst of confusion, yet somehow, we like to pull Him into our mess and expect for Him to clean it up. If we stick to the word of God and follow His commands, we won't have to worry about that.

<u>Scripture Meditation:</u>

1 Peter 2:9-10

But you are not like that, for you are a chosen people. You are royal priests, a holy nation, God's very own possession. As a result, you can show others the goodness of God, for he called you out of the darkness into his wonderful light. Once you had no identity as a people; now you are God's people. Once you received no mercy; now you have received God's mercy.

Ephesians 1:5

God decided in advance to adopt us into his own family by

bringing us to himself through Jesus Christ. This is what he wanted to do, and it gave him great pleasure.

Jeremiah 1:5

"I knew you before I formed you in your mother's womb. Before you were born I set you apart and appointed you as my prophet to the nations."

<u>*Reflection Questions*</u>

1. What do you feel God is saying to you in this chapter?

   ____

   ____

   ____

   ____

2. In the last year, where have you struggled in your identity? For example, have you struggled with understanding who you are in Christ or struggled with being set apart?

   ____

   ____

   ____

   ____

3. With the world telling us all kinds of things about who they think we are, what are a few things you need to keep in prayer to remind yourself of God's word when it comes to identity (i.e. the world saying it's okay to choose your gender or marry someone of the same sex)?

   ____

   ____

   ____

   ____

4. How can you remind yourself of who you are in Christ daily? Other than scriptures to meditate on, is there a practical way you can remind yourself of your identity in Christ (i.e. texting yourself daily, etc.)? Write a few ways below.

____

____

____

____

5

No Games – The Tic-Tac-Toe Effect

Dear God,

I know that You say what You mean and mean what You say. Lately, I feel like I've been playing around with sin and I know that's not Your will for my life. You've made it clear that the wages of sin is death. I don't want to experience a premature death because of temporary pleasures. Father help me to see things from Your perspective. Help me to live a life pleasing to You, no matter how hard it gets. My friends may look like they're having a good time, but I know that in the end, a good time is just that – a good time for a short period of time. In Your word, it says that obedience is better than sacrifice. Help me to avoid trying to put in the good works (going to church, reading my bible and putting on praise and worship), if I'm not going to obey Your word. You don't need my worship at the expense of me being fake. You want my heart. I pray for a new heart. Purify me from the inside out and make me new. Help me to stop playing games and to stop keeping in touch with hell. The enemy is after my soul and my life. I don't want to give him a foothold in my life. I pray for conviction to invade my spirit whenever I'm tempted to sin. I pray the Holy Spirit will have His way in my life by leading me into all truth. What looks good on the surface may not be good for me. I trust You to guide me back to Your truth whenever I go astray. Help me to surrender to You daily.

In Jesus Name, Amen.

Reality Check

I remember my junior year in college at Temple University. I was asked to go out on a date by this guy from my job. He had been pressing me to hang out with him for some time and I eventually gave in. It wasn't that I was scared to tell him 'no', I just didn't see any point in not going out to have a good time with a nice guy. One night, we had just hung up from a pretty dope phone conversation. I threw on my headphones and was listening to gospel music. All of a sudden, I heard, "Do not go out with him." I was so startled by what I heard that I shut the music off and waited to see if I would hear it again. I didn't. But I did call him back and tell him I couldn't go. It wasn't until a year later when I ran into one of our former co-workers on the train that I found out he had a kid and a girlfriend. Based on the child's age, he had been dealing with her while trying to take me out. He had the nerve to make me feel bad when I cancelled on him. What I've learned is that God is the King at Tic-Tac-Toe. If you've played tic-tac-toe any number of times, it can be really frustrating when someone keeps blocking your move. You think you're about to win the game and they've found a way to block your win. A lot of times, God's 'no' comes off a lot like that tic-tac-toe experience. I would play tic-tac-toe for hours with my friends. We'd get a piece of paper and keep on playing until one of us got tired. In life, you will see many tic-tac-toe games throughout your story. You will look back and see where God blocked you from making a move that you thought would lead to a win. He may or may not share with you why He blocked it, but if there's one thing I've learned about God is that He sees further down the line than we do. What we think will end up in success, He knows won't. If God blocks your move, it's for your good. You can't keep playing with sin because eventually, you'll get burned. But if you play God's version of the game, you'll always win.

Scripture Meditation:

Romans 6:23
For the wages of sin is death, but the free gift of God is eternal life through Christ Jesus our Lord.

1 Corinthians 13:12
Now we see things imperfectly, like puzzling reflections in a mirror, but then we will see everything with perfect clarity.[a] All that I know now is partial and incomplete, but then I will know everything completely, just as God now knows me completely.

Acts 16:7
Then coming to the borders of Mysia, they headed north for the province of Bithynia,[a] but again the Spirit of Jesus did not allow them to go there.

1 John 5:18
We know that God's children do not make a practice of sinning, for God's Son holds them securely, and the evil one cannot touch them.

<u>*Reflection Questions*</u>

1. What do you feel God is saying to you in this chapter?

____

____

____

____

2. What are some sins you have knowingly committed that you haven't repented for? I don't want you to feel bad, but this devotional is meant to help you maintain your freedom. Write them out here.

____

____

____

____

3. What are some areas where you still struggle with sin?

____

____

____

____

4. Write down three ways you can hold yourself accountable in these areas. You may need to get an accountability partner.

____

____

____

____

SOPHOMORE YEAR

Here's your first God Girl Challenge. Use your phone to open
the video or download a QR reader from the App store.

6

Switching Lanes

Dear God,

Thank You for the time I've been able to invest in my studies thus far. You've been faithful to see me through. Before I take any more classes, I want to acknowledge this feeling that's been tugging at my heart. I feel led to switch my major. I don't want to lose what I've studied so far, but if I'm honest, I no longer have the same passion for what I'm currently studying. I know this was something I wanted to do before, and I even found myself looking for internships in this space. Unfortunately, I feel a switch in my spirit. I'm not sure what You want me to study moving forward, but I do know that this could mean a completely different area of study. I don't want to assume that this will be easy. This could mean another year in college. I also don't want to assume that you're telling me to go to seminary. The mission field that You have chosen for me doesn't mean I have to go to seminary. Help me to take my time with this decision. I pray for wisdom to invade my mind right now. Help me not to think of all the logical reasons why this won't work out. Help me not to worry about the finances or the things that will be affected by this change. It's okay for me to take inventory but help me not to worry. I trust You to bring me into complete clarity before this next semester starts. Guide my footsteps to Your best for me.

In Jesus name, Amen.

Reality Check

Nobody could've told me that today, I wouldn't be a Pediatrician. I wanted to work in the medical field all my life and I just knew that I was destined to be a doctor. My first two years of college, I studied pre-nursing and took all of the pre-nursing courses I was supposed to take. When I got to Temple University, the advisor let me into the pre-nursing program at Temple, even though I was a few points shy of the required GPA. She extended favor to me. I thought that was a sign that I was where I was supposed to be. When that first semester at Temple ended, I had a 2.97 GPA. I felt like a bomb had fallen on my chest. The agreement was that she would let me in, but I had to maintain a 3.0. I went back to the professor who gave me a B minus asking if she could go back over the last exam we'd taken. I had given a correct answer that if she wanted to be honest about it, she could've accepted it. She wouldn't budge. I was so pissed that I didn't even consider that this was God's first way of trying to get my attention. I decided that I would switch to pre-med instead. Never prayed about it. I just decided all of those science and math courses weren't going to go to waste. But to my surprise, God would continue to allow me to fail until I dropped that major and switched over to Journalism. By failing, I mean getting C's in chemistry when you need at least a B to even be considered for med school. Finally, I made the switch. It was seamless and I couldn't believe how I had pretty much already taken the required courses

I needed for Journalism. I still ended up having to do an extra year, but if I'm honest, it was fun. Never be afraid to switch your major because of money or time invested. God considered all of that before making this request of you. I know some of you may be reading this and wondering why God would *not* tell you your major in the first place. Let's be honest – many of us see signs or hear God's still small voice, but we brush it off or chalk it up to the voice of fear. Sometimes, it may be fear, but it could also be God sending you a warning sign. This prayer is meant to encourage those who didn't pull God into their decision in the first place or who feels a gnawing in their spirit to change lanes. Sometimes, God will allow us to go down the path we chose knowing that we'll hit a dead end anyway. Ultimately, that will bring us back to Him. Just remember, God wastes nothing. Those science and math courses I took, still counted towards my degree.

Scripture Meditation:

Proverbs 19:21
You can make many plans, but the Lord's purpose will prevail.

Proverbs 16:9
We can make our plans, but the Lord determines our steps.

Romans 8:28
And we know that God causes everything to work together for the good of those who love God and are called according to his purpose for them.

Proverbs 3:5-6
Trust in the Lord with all your heart; do not depend on your

own understanding. Seek his will in all you do, and he will show you which path to take.

Reflection Questions

1. What do you feel God is saying to you in this chapter?

____

____

____

____

2. Did you seek God's will when you started applying for college? If not, why?

____

____

____

____

3. How have you included God in your decisions since starting college? If you haven't, what's stopping you?

____

____

____

____

4. How can you be sure that God is included in your day-to-day (not just college life) moving forward? What are some practical things you can do starting now?

____

____

____

____

7

Dateless and Sexless

Dear God,

It's another lonely night in my dorm room. All my friends have gone out on dates or they are hanging out at parties. I don't understand why I can't go, but I didn't have peace about it, so here I am. I want to be honest with You. Sometimes, I don't see the harm in going out to a party to have a little fun or going on a date. I want to continue to follow Your commandments and not put myself in the way of temptation, but it's getting harder and harder. I get that I should wait until marriage to have sex, but is dating so wrong? I need Your help with this. I want to serve and please You, but I'm tired of feeling alone. It's hard being one of the few college students that sits in her dorm room on a Friday night. I feel unseen, unheard and unwanted. I believe if You told me not to go, then it's for a reason. I'm asking for Your strength to obey what You've told me to do. Sometimes, I don't even know why You're telling me to say 'no', but I know that I should. I'm tired of my friends asking me questions about why I don't do certain things. It makes me feel like a child. Please give me Your perspective on this matter. Help me not to give into temptation. Help me to obey Your word, even if I have to stand alone. Lead me to friends who are just like me – friends who are pursuing their relationship with You, who are practicing abstinence and who are putting You first in all things. I speak peace over my life, and I believe at the right time, if You have someone You want me to meet in college, You will lead us to each other. He will respect my values and my relationship with You. Give me peace and help me to bask in Your love.

In Jesus name, Amen.

Reality Check

You knew this chapter was coming. It's one of the hardest things for young women who are in college to face. You want to have fun and enjoy your college years, but there are things your friends do that you know is wrong. The reason why I started this prayer off with a raw, honest conversation between you and God is because I know that God doesn't want you to be fake. He wants you to pour your heart out in the most honest way. He knows walking in purity and obedience isn't easy. He never said it would be. He also knows the way you feel before you tell Him, so coming to Him with a cute little prayer that doesn't fully open your heart to Him isn't what He wants. He's your Father. He wants you to talk to Him and reveal what's really in your heart. When I was in college, I was having sex. But there were times when I felt so alone, and I didn't have anyone asking me to go out on dates. I struggled to be abstinent in college and if I'm honest, I wasn't even really trying. But when I did step back from the dating scene and from having sex, it was as if God had reached down and wrapped me in His arms, pulling me away from the dangers of sin. Yet somehow, I broke free when loneliness would constrict at my heart again. At the time of me writing this book, I have not dated or had sex in four years. When loneliness constricts at my heart, I have to run to my word, pray and sometimes, I even have to text one of my accountability partners. I have things in place to help me not feel like I'm about to break my promise to God and myself. Is it easy? Absolutely not. But I think about young women like you who need modern day examples of women who are living what they preach.

I still struggled with masturbation from 2018 to 2019. While I wasn't having sex, I was still sinning just by touching myself. But God had a solution for that. He told me to go to therapy in the spring of 2020. Through my therapy sessions at that time, I ended up healing from the childhood wound of when I was touched at four. God revealed to me that that was why I still struggled in this area. I had forgiven the person who violated me, but I hadn't truly healed the wound. Sometimes, when we're struggling to break free of sin, God wants us to get to the root. Had I dealt with this wound in college, I would've been stronger in this area. Instead of feeling sorry for yourself that you aren't out at a party or that you don't have a date, spend some time with God asking Him if there's any areas in your life that need His touch. Being dateless and sexless doesn't have to be morbid. Turn those date nights into spending time with God, yourself and dealing with your past trauma. You don't want these things to come up later when you are ready to date and cause issues in your relationship. Trust God with your dating and sex life and let Him bless you with a love you won't ever regret.

Scripture Meditation:

1 Thessalonians 4:3-4

God's will is for you to be holy, so stay away from all sexual sin. Then each of you will control his own body and live in holiness and honor—

Galatians 5:19-21

When you follow the desires of your sinful nature, the results are very clear: sexual immorality, impurity, lustful pleasures, idolatry, sorcery, hostility, quarreling, jealousy, outbursts of anger, selfish ambition, dissension, division, envy, drunkenness, wild parties, and other sins like these. Let me tell you again, as I have before, that anyone living that sort of life will not inherit the Kingdom of God.

1 Corinthians 6:19

Don't you realize that your body is the temple of the Holy Spirit, who lives in you and was given to you by God? You do not belong to yourself,

Song of Solomon 2:7

Promise me, O women of Jerusalem, by the gazelles and wild deer, not to awaken love until the time is right.

<u>*Reflection Questions*</u>

1. What do you feel God is saying to you in this chapter?

____

____

____

____

2. Have you had your eye on somebody on campus? Write down what has attracted you to them. If not, write down the kind of guy you would find attractive (not just looks).

____

____

____

____

3. If this guy approached you today, would you be able to date honorably? If so, what steps would you take to be sure you wouldn't compromise your values? Be honest.

____

____

____

____

4. If you've already started dating, re-read the scriptures listed in this chapter. Have you been living a life that honors God based on these scriptures alone? Explain.

____

____

____

____

8

It's Just TV, right?

Dear God,

I know that I've been watching, listening to and reading things that may not be pleasing to You. While I just believe I'm enjoying life, You have very specific instructions on how we are supposed to live our life here on earth. Things we may see as fun, may not be pleasing to You and could actually be more harmful than we think. I ask You to take over my entertainment choices from this day forward. Help me to help myself by not second guessing that feeling in my spirit that arises when I'm watching my favorite show, listening to my favorite artist or reading my favorite magazine. I know that we can't lock ourselves in the house and hide from the evils of the world, but we can control what we bring into our homes. Please forgive me for not bringing this to You sooner and for feeling like I can hide certain aspects of my life from You. Your Word is very clear about trying the spirits and being obedient to You. This means, trying the spirits behind all forms of entertainment. Help me not to view it as "just a song" or "just TV" but to view it as "If Jesus was sitting next to me, would I be watching or listening to this?". I long to please You and to keep my heart and life pure. Not perfection, but progress. Help me to realize there are fun things I can watch, listen to and read, without it offending You. Help me not to grieve the Holy Spirit and to understand that this life is not my own. Help me not to be influenced by those around me who would try and convince me that "it's okay" and who tell me that "YOLO". The one time I live, I choose to live for God. I also pray that You raise up Your sons and daughters who long to be in the entertainment field and open doors for them so that they can create content that is led by You. Lord, I love having fun, I love going to concerts and I love watching movies. Help me choose things that aren't going to make me feel weighed down, but that are going to lift me up. At times, we watch and listen to things that seem okay, but we don't even realize the spirit that is attached to it. A sad song that brings about a spirit of sadness or a love song that makes us yearn for that ex you told us to cut off. It all has a spirit and I ask that You keep me covered. Your angels encamp around me, and I will continue to pursue the entertainment that You would have me to pursue. In Jesus Name, Amen.

Reality Check

I know. It's only entertainment. You watch your favorite shows without any concern for whether or not God would be okay with it. And sometimes, you know the answer, but you convince yourself that it's just "TV" and it's not "that bad". You hear your voice, but the voice of God keeps pressing in, trying to get your attention. And you reason with your voice. Strangely enough, this has happened to me on numerous occasions. My struggle has always been that I'm a writer. I write novels, TV scripts and film scripts. I didn't think there was anything wrong with what I was watching. Of course, I knew sexual content was wrong, but I felt like if it didn't have sex in it, then there was nothing wrong with it. But God convicted me when I was watching a show with a lot of cursing. It was as if He knew I was longing to hear His voice in every area of my life. I realized that watching anything that is obscene or offensive to God, should be offensive to us.

That brings me to shows like *Harlem, Good Trouble* and *Queens.* Many of today's shows have way too much sexual content in them. Before we even get to the end of the first episode, we've seen so much nudity that we forget the show's premise. When I was growing up, they went to the bedroom. You may have seen a bra or a pair of boxers, but that was it. You didn't get to see what they show now, and they are showing it with no problem on network television. This isn't even cable, and it's not always after dark. Today, I'm not sure I would let my children watch television if I had any. In order for us to help ourselves, we have to be willing to hear what God is telling us and decide to act on it immediately. I start my day off with worship music, devotions and prayer. I spend about an hour in the morning with God and then again at night. I also pray throughout the day and pull out my favorite scriptures to keep me encouraged. If I'm not connected with God on a moment-by-moment basis, I feel lost. When I'm watching TV, I'm always in tune to how my spirit man feels. If something keeps nagging at me, I turn it off. Sometimes, God just wants a season. I remember when God asked me to turn off reality shows earlier in 2015. I didn't watch reality TV for about three months, and *Love & Hip Hop* and *Real Housewives of Atlanta* were both on!

But it was refreshing. Hearing those women curse at each other every other moment and seeing men berate their women on national television had me jaded for a minute. At times, God will test us to see if we're willing to give something up for Him and it's not always permanent. If you can honestly say if God asked you to give up a magazine, a favorite artist or TV show, without you knowing whether it would be permanent or not, you would hesitate or you would say no, you need to check whether you're saved or not. I think it's safe to say while the Bible doesn't outright say anything about entertainment, it speaks very clearly on darkness, walking in integrity and setting our eyes on things that have worth. I think that speaks more volumes than something that would outright say "Don't watch movies with cursing and violence" or "Don't listen to sexual song lyrics". These verses actually make you think and choose wisely based on your own judgment. Isn't God an awesome God? He's not going to force you to do anything. He's going to drop the wisdom jewels for you and let you decide.

Scripture Meditation:

Psalm 101:2-3
I will be careful to live a blameless life— when will you come to help me? I will lead a life of integrity in my own home. I will refuse to look at anything vile and vulgar. I hate all who deal crookedly; I will have nothing to do with them.

Ephesians 5:11
Take no part in the worthless deeds of evil and darkness; instead, expose them.

Titus 2:12
And we are instructed to turn from godless living and sinful pleasures. We should live in this evil world with wisdom, righteousness, and devotion to God.

Proverbs 4:23

Guard your heart above all else, for it determines the course of your life.

<u>*Reflection Questions*</u>

1. What do you feel God is saying to you in this chapter?

____

____

____

____

2. What television shows or music have you been listening to that you know is displeasing to God?

____

____

____

____

3. Analyze the last three shows you watched (or songs you listened to). What things jump out at you as sin or things that can be perceived as darkness according to God's standards?

____

____

____

____

4. There's a resource guide in the back of this book that lists movies, music and entertainment suitable for a believer. Explain how you will make the shift to please God with your entertainment choices from here on out. Be intentional.

____

____

____

____

9

Sorority Life

Dear God,

I desire community and I have my eyes on a sorority here on campus. I've heard so many stories about why it's good to pledge in a sorority, but I want to be honest about this decision. I long to be a part of something bigger than me. I desire to be popular and I know that being connected to these group of women will soothe the lonely feelings I have when it comes to friendships and help me with my networking. However, I don't want to be naïve to the negative things I've heard as well. I've seen videos on YouTube of people denouncing their sororities and fraternities, I've heard testimonies of people who felt conflicted because they knew they should've never pledged, and I've heard stories of hazing that I know you would not subject me to. Is it so wrong to be a member of a powerful organization that gives back? I want to do what pleases You and not what sounds good to society or my community. I know there are a plethora of ways to give back without joining a sorority.

I know that I can find community without joining a sorority and I know that You will reveal me to the world when it's my time. Trying to win popularity isn't the goal. Help me with this decision. I want to build with likeminded women, and I want to also connect with the organizations here on campus. Show me where to go. Show me who to talk to. Lead me to what would please You, even if my flesh kicks and screams all the way there. I want to serve You with every area of my life. If You don't open this door, help me to see that it's for my good and that You have a way for me to connect with powerful, amazing people without going through a process that would dehumanize me. I trust Your guidance.

In Jesus name, Amen.

Reality Check

I know. I know. You didn't want to read this prayer. If you're honest, you've probably already talked to at least two sororities since you've been on campus. You've seen the fliers inviting you to their programs or you've seen the flyer inviting you to the rush. You get excited thinking about getting your "letters" and being invited into an illustrious organization that's known all over the world. I went out for a sorority twice. Once in undergrad and once in grad. Let me just tell you this: When God says no, He means it. To be honest, I didn't know when I didn't make it in undergrad, that it was because God was saying 'no'. I had prayed about it, but I prayed that I would get in. When I overheard someone talking about the secret rush, I knew that this was my moment. I showed up. Even won a prize. I did everything I was supposed to do, only to be told my transcripts never made it. Then, in grad school, I tried again. This time, I made it to the interview process, but I still didn't get in. It wasn't until a few years ago that I realized God was protecting me the entire time.

I am in no way, shape or form disrespecting or coming against the Divine Nine or any other sorority that exists. What I am saying is that God will not share His throne with anyone. From what I've learned since then, many of these organizations do take parts of the Bible and incorporate them into their rituals and their books. I've seen a video of a former member of a sorority denouncing her sorority and literally highlighting from the books and rituals they recited, how the organization took scriptures from the bible and inserted their organization name where God's name was. Listen, this isn't gossip – this is real verifiable information (go to YouTube and watch any number of the videos where someone has denounced Greek Life). I believe in His loving way, God protected me from joining the sorority. You might ask, "Well why wouldn't He stop others from joining them? There are Christians that are in these organizations." But who says He didn't try to stop them? Remember, when our hearts are already set, we tend to pray in the direction of what we want instead of praying for God's will to be done.

I never once asked God if this was something that He wanted for me. I prayed that I would get in and that He would provide the money to join. If I'm honest, I barely even included Him in that. We have to realize that many times, God will send us warnings – like those YouTube videos – or even just us not making it to the next round. Remember, He never wants us confused about anything in our lives. This doesn't mean confusion won't come, but for the most part, when you want to serve God and do His will, He will make a way for you to do so. If you've already joined a sorority, don't feel condemned. Pray. Ask God what He wants you to do from here. Don't push away the voice telling you to denounce (if that's what He leads you to do). Don't try to hear what you want to hear. Take it before God and let Him lead you out the way He sees fit.

While sorority life is painted as fun and exciting, there is also a dark side. No matter what people try to tell you, anything secretive is rooted in some form of darkness. This doesn't mean they are bad people or that the organizations as a whole are bad, but you have to research and know the root of everything you want to attach yourself to. Don't be surprise at what God asks you to give up.

<u>*Scripture Meditation:*</u>

Luke 8:14

The seeds that fell among the thorns represent those who hear the message, but all too quickly the message is crowded out by the cares and riches and pleasures of this life. And so they never grow into maturity.

1 Corinthians 6:12

You say, "I am allowed to do anything"—but not everything is good for you. And even though "I am allowed to do anything," I must not become a slave to anything.

Exodus 20:3-4

You must not have any other god but me. You must not make for yourself an idol of any kind or an image of anything in the heavens or on the earth or in the sea.

Matthew 6:24

No one can serve two masters. For you will hate one and love the other; you will be devoted to one and despise the other. You cannot serve God and be enslaved to money.

<u>*Reflection Questions*</u>

1. What do you feel God is saying to you in this chapter?

____

____

____

____

2. If you're interested in joining a sorority, list three reasons why below. If not, list why you don't want to join one.

____

____

____

____

3. If you've already started the process to join, list what you believe God is saying to you now.

____

____

____

____

4. If you're a member, did this chapter convict you? List some things that came up if so.

____

____

____

____

IO

The Despair of Comparison

Dear God,

I find myself looking to my left and right on a regular basis. I see my friends soaring in their classes and making the Dean's list. My friends are dating and having a good time in life. I honestly feel left out. I'm struggling in a few of my classes and I'm doing my best to maintain my GPA. If I'm honest God, sometimes it feels like You're blessing my friends and leaving me to struggle. Most of the time, they forget all about You and barely serve You like I do. What am I doing wrong? I know I shouldn't see my friends as rivals and that I shouldn't compare myself to them, but it's hard not to feel overlooked when you're doing everything right but can't seem to get ahead. Please direct my attention and my heart back to You. Help me not to lose hope knowing that You perfect everything that concerns me. I know the enemy is a liar and he's trying to cause division in my friendships just by planting negative thoughts of jealousy in my mind. I don't want to be jealous of those I love. Help me with these feelings, Lord. Show me where I may be stumbling and keep me from having a self-righteous attitude. I don't know what my friends do in their private time with You. Forgive me for assuming that I deserve something for walking in Your ways. You call us to walk in Your ways because it's good for us, not so we can get the things we want. I don't want to fall into the trap of despair because I'm comparing my life to others. Help me out of this pit of darkness and keep me guarded.

In Jesus name, Amen.

<u>*Reality Check*</u>

This was me in college. Super self-righteous and always trying to pick apart someone's walk with God. I would be in church several times a week, serving and giving up my weeknights for Christ. When I was back on campus, I'd see friends of mine who loved God, but weren't doing as much as me (so I assumed) getting blessed left and right. It was so hard feeling like I had been forgotten by God. The truth is, when these feelings come, the enemy is trying to keep our eyes on things that don't matter to God. He's not interested in who "acts" more Christian. God always looks at the heart. If we're consistently measuring ourselves against other humans, we will always miss the mark. The only mark we should be trying to reach is the mark of the high calling in Christ Jesus. Comparison doesn't just take place on social media. When I was in college, there was only Facebook and MySpace. My struggle came with walking on campus and living life in real time. One of the things that helped me was understanding that my friend's journeys were going to be different from mine. We may take some of the same classes and maybe even one or two of us have the same major, but essentially, our paths will be different. I also learned that comparison was killing my drive. It was causing me to suffer mentally when I didn't have to. It was also causing a wedge to come in between me and my friends. Why? Because even though I would never verbally express what I was feeling, the things I was thinking was causing me to push them away and they had done nothing wrong. They were living. I saw something on social media a few years ago and I've held it near and dear to my heart ever since. I hope it sets you free. "You should never be jealous of another woman. God may want to do more for you than He did for her." Now, this isn't about comparing how much you get versus how much she get, but it puts things in perspective. Sometimes our path is harder because the blessings are bigger. If we want someone else's glory, we'd have to also go through the hell part of their story. That's why I never envy another person's anointing or platform. I have no idea what hell they had to go through to get to where they are. Don't fall into despair because of comparison. Guard your eyes, heart and whatever else you need to in order to stay humble before the Lord. He'll exalt you in due time.

<u>Scripture Meditation:</u>

Galatians 1:10
Obviously, I'm not trying to win the approval of people, but of God. If pleasing people were my goal, I would not be Christ's servant.

Psalm 139:14
Thank you for making me so wonderfully complex! Your workmanship is marvelous—how well I know it.

Isaiah 45:9
"What sorrow awaits those who argue with their Creator. Does a clay pot argue with its maker? Does the clay dispute with the one

who shapes it, saying, 'Stop, you're doing it wrong!' Does the pot exclaim, 'How clumsy can you be?'

Hebrews 13:5
Don't love money; be satisfied with what you have. For God has said, "I will never fail you. I will never abandon you."

Reflection Questions

1. What do you feel God is saying to you in this chapter?

____

____

____

____

2. How have you been comparing yourself to another girl lately? How is this not pleasing to God?

____

____

____

____

3. List five things you love about yourself below.

____

____

____

____

4. How can you focus on the things that you love about yourself when you feel led to compare (text them to yourself, write them on a vision board, etc.)?

____

____

____

____

JUNIOR YEAR

Here's your second God Girl Challenge. Use your phone to open the video or download a QR reader from the App store.

I I

Mirror, Mirror on The Wall

Dear God,

I'm sorry for ever thinking of myself as less than someone else. I desire to be a better person, but I should never look to my right or left and envy what someone else looks like, has or what you are doing in their lives. Please help me boost my confidence in myself. I know that starts with my confidence in You. I am made in Your image and likeness therefore, I am amazing, inside and out. I am fearfully and wonderfully made. There is nobody on earth like me, and that is powerful alone! You know the number of hairs on my head and you knew the plans that you had for me before I was in my mother's womb. You knew me. You believe in me and there is no reason that I shouldn't believe in myself. Help me spend more time appreciating the great things about myself and not focusing on the areas where I need work. This includes my image, my hair, my clothes and my body. Those things don't define who I am or who You've called me to be. Help me remember that You always look at the heart and that is where true beauty lies. I thank You right now that I see myself as beautiful, fearless and priceless. Help me become a strong Proverbs 31 woman that can't be touched by the enemy. I love You and I love myself.

In Jesus name, Amen.

Reality Check

The number of young girls who look at the cover of a magazine and question their worth really breaks my heart. One, it's a trick of the enemy to make you think you're worthless and have no place in the world. He enjoys seeing God's brightest creation wonder if they will ever be pretty enough, bright enough, loved enough and just enough, period. The sad part is, it all started with Eve. I believe since that day in the garden the enemy got a kick out of seeing how he can wiggle into the mind of the woman. Notice he didn't even try Adam. He knew that the woman was an easier target. This isn't because we're weak, but we are built with an emotional sensor that can be easily reached. Because we're so fragile, we tend to be harder on ourselves and work on constant improvement. I haven't met one woman who isn't working on something, whether it's weight loss, changing her hair, planning a wedding, having a baby, getting that big promotion at work – you name it. Especially if they're single and don't have children.

God loves progress but there's no such thing as perfection. What a lot of reality shows emulate when it comes to body image is perfection. They all have the perfect boobs, a round bottom and pretty faces. Even the roughest looking female on a reality show has a body that would send Jessica Rabbit running to hide, and although most of them may admit that they have implants, young girls watching forget that bit of information as they watch men swooning over these women. I don't believe that getting plastic surgery means you have low self-esteem, but I do believe that changing every part of your body or certain parts for more attention from men says a lot about how you view yourself. I remember feeling like I was too skinny. I was in high school thinking of ways to grow curves. I had some weight in elementary school, but somewhere between seventh and tenth grade, it seemed to disappear, which was weird because I ate a lot in middle and high school. As boys started to pay more attention to me, I found myself always comparing my body to someone else's. I hated walking down the street with friends of mine who were thicker than me. Even if guys thought I was prettier, it was the one with the body that got all the attention.

And having dark skin didn't help. I had to hear that famous line "You're cute, for a dark skin girl," whenever I did get a guy's attention. Now I must say, after seeing Nia Long in *Boyz N The Hood* when I was seven, I really fell in love with my skin. I felt like she gave dark skin sisters a reason to put an extra switch in their hips. So even when guys would say that, I didn't have an issue with my complexion, but the weight thing continued to wear on me mentally. I would research pills at GNC when I was in high school to see which ones would make me thicker. My mom was so tired of hearing me talk about a problem she didn't feel even mattered. I was determined to be thick. I never took anything to increase my body weight, but somehow when I got to college, I noticed that I evened out nicely. I think I was around twenty when I started to embrace my body more. I realized that there would always be somebody thicker, somebody with a bigger butt and somebody whose skin was prettier. If I didn't learn to love myself, even if I had the body, I wouldn't find anyone else to love me either. Plus, those aren't the kind of guys I wanted anyway. If they only went for my friends for their bodies, that's what would keep them around – a body.

But that didn't mean that I somehow didn't long for the attention. I really didn't start to love myself until I was about twenty-three. I started to see the need for self-love when I started attaching myself to people just because of their looks. Knowing you're pretty and believing it are two different things. While I never felt I was ugly, everyone has a complex and controlling it is important. Chrisette Michele has a song called "Visual Love" off her *Better* album. That song speaks volumes. Visual Love is a false sense of love that is rooted in selfishness, but it doesn't just apply to choosing a mate. A lot of people are caught up in "visual" escapades. Instagram has proven that. People are jealous of lifestyle's they see posted that don't even exist. People are jealous of couples that issues will never be posted online because most people won't post their struggles. That's why it's important to know who you are and WHOSE you are. When you value who God made you to be, you don't need validation from social media, people or a man. Learn to validate yourself and appreciate what you have to offer the world.

It starts with identifying your self-worth and owning it. I began to tell myself that my worth was priceless and that if God saw me as a princess, then there was no way I would let even my own insecurities tell me anything different. In this day and age, you have to speak over your life for every area of your life. You have to catch those feelings before they start to get rooted in your heart. Will you have your days? Absolutely. Everyone has days where they don't feel like they are 100% themselves. We're human. But dwelling on those negative feelings will only make you feel worse. Write some affirmations for yourself. Here's some to get your started. Make them personal and own them when you say them. I recorded affirmations on my phone and sometimes, I would play them at night while I was falling asleep. Hearing your voice repeat positive sayings about yourself definitely gets ingrained in your mind.

Positive Self-Affirmations:

- I am 360 degrees of beautiful – inside, outside and all around.
- I love everything about me and what I don't like, God is changing for the better. Even my flaws will work out for my good.
- I am bold, fearless and I accept myself for who I am, right now.
- I accept compliments with a smile and I only say nice things about myself daily.
- I own my pretty and bask in my uniqueness.

These are just a few. What positive things can you say about yourself right now? Add those to the list and get to affirming.

Scripture Meditation:

1 Peter 3:3-4

Don't be concerned about the outward beauty of fancy hairstyles, expensive jewelry, or beautiful clothes. You should clothe yourselves instead with the beauty that comes from within, the unfading beauty of a gentle and quiet spirit, which is so precious to God.

Ephesians 2:10

For we are God's masterpiece. He has created us anew in Christ Jesus, so we can do the good things he planned for us long ago.

Song of Solomon 4:7

You are altogether beautiful, my darling, beautiful in every way.

1 Samuel 16:7

But the Lord said to Samuel, "Don't judge by his appearance or height, for I have rejected him. The Lord doesn't see things the way you see them. People judge by outward appearance, but the Lord looks at the heart."

Reflection Questions

1. What do you feel God is saying to you in this chapter?

____

____

____

____

2. When you look at yourself in the mirror, what are the first three words that come to mind?

____

____

____

____

3. How do you define beauty?

____

____

____

____

4. List three things you can say to yourself that are based on God's word whenever you start to question your appearance.

____

____

____

____

12

Integrity is a Muscle

Dear God,

I've known all my life that I'm different. When others wanted to do things that weren't okay, even when I didn't understand why I was saying 'no', I knew I was doing the right thing. Right now, I feel like my integrity is being tested. There are things that I wouldn't normally do, but is it wrong to cheat on a test if my friend says I can look at her paper during the exam? Is it so wrong to have a guy helping me with my bills if we don't go all the way? I mean, I'm not really hurting anyone, am I? I know that You're big on character and You want Your children to do things that align with Your character. I'm having a hard time with this because I feel like life has gotten a little easier since I've started taking shortcuts. I know there's no little or big sin, but I'm trying not to get comfortable just because it doesn't seem to be hurting anyone. Father, give me the courage and wisdom to obey You no matter what. Help me to know that sin comes in a little at a time and can eventually cost me my life. Even if

I don't see physical repercussions right away, I'm spiritually hurting myself and grieving Your heart. Help me to continue to honor You, even when it's hard. I know that every time I do something wrong or right, it plants a seed. The seed I water determines the harvest I will receive. Help me to plant good seeds and trust them to produce a good harvest in due season. Help me to not get weary in well-doing knowing that I'll reap a harvest if I faint not. Help me to uproot any bad seeds I've sown by calling out my sin to You. Help bring any areas to the surface I've previously overlooked because it didn't seem that bad. Help me to maintain my integrity by remembering that You've given me all things that pertain to life and godliness. I want to serve You with every area of my life.

In Jesus Name, Amen.

Reality Check

I prided myself on having integrity in college. So whenever something happened where my integrity was called into question, I was bummed. It had taken me quite some time to really become mature in this area, so I fought to keep it. That's not to say I was perfect, but I did my best to maintain my integrity. I remember when I was studying pre-nursing at Community College of Philadelphia and one of my professors had just given me back an exam. I didn't do well on the exam at all. Everyone was in the hallway talking about it after class. I heard some people saying how they appreciated that the person sitting next to them let them cheat. I wasn't shocked, but I definitely couldn't believe they would discuss it right outside of the classroom. One of the girls in the class started walking with me and she was talking about the cheating and how hard the class was. For some reason, I explained to her that I didn't cheat. I didn't let people cheat off of me either. Instead of judging me, she said she appreciated me for being honest and that she would never look off my paper. Then, there was a time that following semester where I did let someone look off my paper. We will all have struggles in this area. Just because nobody is looking doesn't mean God isn't watching. If we perform for an audience of One at all times, we'll more than likely make wiser decisions. God will often place you in situations where you can flex your integrity muscle on purpose. He wants to test you in this area to see what He can trust you with in the next season. Trust me – this is challenging. I never asked God to trust me, but for some reason, He does and to show me how much He does, He puts me in situations where I have a choice to honor Him or to do what pleases my flesh. I always choose Him, even when it hurts, but again, this came with growth over time. If you're struggling in this area, don't beat yourself up. It took me a while to really find my footing. My college years were filled with me convincing myself that I wasn't really sinning because it was only oral sex, or we were only making out. But what we have to consider in these situations is that the enemy only needs an inch. Once he has a foothold in any area of your life, he can create a stronghold. This makes deliverance and healing so much harder and for most of us, we've already been dealt a hard hand in life. There's no need to make it harder.

Scripture Meditation:

Proverbs 11:3
Honesty guides good people; dishonesty destroys treacherous people.

Proverbs 28:6
Better to be poor and honest than to be dishonest and rich.

1 Peter 3:16
But do this in a gentle and respectful way. Keep your conscience

clear. Then if people speak against you, they will be ashamed when they see what a good life you live because you belong to Christ.

Proverbs 12:22

The Lord detests lying lips, but he delights in those who tell the truth.

<u>Reflection Questions</u>

1. What do you feel God is saying to you in this chapter?

____

____

____

____

2. Why do you believe God values integrity so much?

____

____

____

____

3. Name a time you did something that went against your integrity. How did God correct you in that situation?

____

____

____

____

4. How can you implement new strategies to walk in integrity starting today? For example, whenever someone is gossiping about someone, I will either get up and leave or tell them that this isn't right and change the subject.

____

____

____

____

13

When Friends Sin

Dear God,

I want to lift up my sister in Christ to You today. She's doing things that aren't pleasing to You and before I jump to judgment, only You know what's going on in her heart. I pray Lord that You would lead her back to You. I pray that You would give her the courage to turn away from sin and keep her eyes on You. I know that this life can be lonely, but during those times, we have to remember that You will provide friendships and relationships for us that are pleasing to You. Humble me to be able to see her the way You see her and to remove any judgmental thoughts from my mind. I could easily be in her shoes and I would want her to pray for me. Re-direct her footsteps toward You. Let her know that she's never too far gone and that You'll leave the ninety-nine to go after the one. Remind her of how precious she is to You. Help me to find encouraging words to say to her during this time. Help me not to give up on her. I may be the only friend she has that can be a light during this dark season. I do ask that You help me to create boundaries so that I don't end up going down the same path. I don't want to be naïve and think that I can hang with her every day and not be tempted to do what she's doing. While I don't look down on her, I have to also be wise. While I'm pouring into her, send me friends that can pour into me. Send relationships that will keep me uplifted and encouraged during this time. Continue to open her eyes and show her more of who You are. Help her have a smooth transition out of relationships and friendships that are a detriment to her life. I pray protection, peace and strength over my friend today. Remove the veil from her eyes so she can be led into truth.

In Jesus name, Amen.

Reality Check

There will be seasons where you will have to pray for a friend and take a step back. This may hurt to hear, but we all have that one friend that's still one-foot in, one-foot out. She loves God, but the fruit of her life shows something totally different. I went through this myself and there were friends that had to back away from me. If I'm honest, they did me a huge favor. Never be afraid to take a step back. Sometimes, this will make your friend realize that something is missing that she needs. In my opinion, our college years are the years where our faith is tested the most. I believe this is because we're away from our parents and our safety net. God wants to strengthen our faith and the enemy wants to break us down. Your flesh will always be in daily competition with your spirit. This is why it's important to stay in God's word daily. This isn't to say temptation won't come, but there were plenty of times I was able to flee "sin" because a scripture came to mind at the right time. The best thing you can do for your friend is pray over her mind and spirit daily. Pray that God will provide ways for her to encounter

Him like she never has before. I also believe God tests our faith in college so that we can develop our own relationship with Him. Most times, when we're raised in the church, we're really eating off of our parent's faith. But when we're out on our own, this gives us a chance to develop our own relationship with God and truly get to know Him for ourselves. Your friend is testing the waters, trying to find her own spiritual rhythm. The key is to encourage her, love her and pray for her. But again, be wise. Boundaries are very important during a time like this. I tried to play the 'hero' way too many times to my friends and would end up falling myself. You can't help someone in an area that you're still struggling in. You can hold each other accountable, but once someone starts to fall in this area, it's best to step back and offer prayer.

<u>Scripture Meditation:</u>

Ecclesiastes 4:9-10
Two people are better off than one, for they can help each other succeed. If one person falls, the other can reach out and help. But someone who falls alone is in real trouble.

Proverbs 27:17
As iron sharpens iron, so a friend sharpens a friend.

Proverbs 13:20
Walk with the wise and become wise; associate with fools and get in trouble.

1 Corinthians 15:33
Don't be fooled by those who say such things, for "bad company corrupts good character."

Reflection Questions

1. What do you feel God is saying to you in this chapter?

____

____

____

____

2. Is there a friend that you can pray for right now who is struggling with sin that you've taken a step back from? List her name and a prayer here.

____

____

____

____

3. Are you the friend that's struggling with sin? Maybe some of your friends are trying to get your attention. Write some of the things they've said to encourage you that you may have been disregarding.

____

____

____

____

4. How can you encourage a friend that is struggling with sin right now? Maybe this is someone that God hasn't told you to step back from, but you want to encourage her before it gets too late.

____

____

____

____

14

Outside the Classroom

Dear God,

I know that I'm focused on finishing my college courses so that I can obtain my degree, but I feel led to start working on a business. I believe in building outside of the classroom. I have an idea that I want to implement, but if I'm honest, I'm nervous. I've seen successful stories about entrepreneurs making it in college and I've seen some that are frightening. I don't want to move too fast, but I know that I don't have to wait until I graduate to pursue my entrepreneurial dreams. Direct me to the best idea that can help me build a profitable, Kingdom business while I'm in school. If I have a desire to do so, then I trust that You placed that desire there. I want to build generational wealth for my family and the things I'm learning now, can help me to do that. As a student, I have access to plenty of resources that others may not have access to. I pray that You'll not only confirm the business idea You want me to develop, but that You'll also send the resources needed to help me get started.

Just like You told the Prophet Jeremiah, you are never too young to do what God has placed in your heart. I trust that because You knew me before You formed me in my mother's womb, You know that I can handle being a student and an entrepreneur at the same time. Give me the grace and wisdom to pace myself. I don't want to move too fast. Give me a strong why so that on the days the vision seems to be taking forever, I can lean on that why and Your will. Help me to launch this business with the least amount of money so that I can capitalize off of my financial resources later. Send destiny helpers that understand the vision and the assignment. I thank You in advance for trusting me to build the ark You've assigned to me.

In Jesus name, Amen.

Reality Check

I think the entrepreneurial bug bit me when I was in middle school. I remember having to sell three boxes of candy bars for my drill team. My mom was so proud of me for selling every last bar before the deadline. My mother has sold Avon ever since I was a toddler. I would help her pack her orders and even help her sell items to some of my classmates. When things like this happen in your life, take note of them. God is giving you signs about what you're called to do. Even if you don't start right away, it's important not to disregard your skills or the skills people give you compliments on just because you may not know what to do with them just yet. God will guide you as you trust Him in this area. I've had several businesses. Some have had a low level of success and others just failed. But one thing I've learned is how to build a business from scratch. I don't take that lightly. That's a skillset not a lot of people have. There are people who will always be an employee simply because they have no desire to build anything, and that's okay. But for you, if you feel that tug in your spirit to start a business, don't feel that you have to wait until you graduate from college. God may want you to lay the foundation for the business now, because He has people lined up to work for you when you graduate. Never put off something you can do today just because you can't see the entire vision today. God's clues are the blueprint you need to get started. Start where you are and let Him guide you the rest of the way. Who knows? Maybe by the time you graduate, you'll have a full-fledged business that's profitable. Even if you only make a few thousand dollars every month, that's enough to start building your life. That way, if you don't snag a job in your major or you just don't feel led to work for anyone when you do graduate, you'll have a stream of income.

Scripture Meditation:

Proverbs 14:23
Work brings profit, but mere talk leads to poverty!

Proverbs 21:5
Good planning and hard work lead to prosperity, but hasty shortcuts lead to poverty.

Deuteronomy 8:17-18
He did all this so you would never say to yourself, 'I have achieved this wealth with my own strength and energy.' Remember the Lord your God. He is the one who gives you power to be successful, in order to fulfill the covenant He confirmed to your ancestors with an oath.

Titus 3:14
Our people must learn to do good by meeting the urgent needs of others; then they will not be unproductive.

Reflection Questions

1. What do you feel God is saying to you in this chapter?

____

____

____

____

2. Do you feel that God is giving you a desire for entrepreneurship? Why or why not?

____

____

____

____

3. What are some things that get you excited about entrepreneurship?

____

____

____

____

4. If you have a business idea, write it down here. Pray over it daily and ask God to give you direction.

____

____

____

____

15

Choosing Friendships

Dear God,

Father, I ask that you help me to choose my friends wisely in this season. Help me to understand that not everyone can go with me on this journey. Just because we have years in or we went to high school together, doesn't mean that this is someone that you want a part of this season. Help me to see that choosing based on Your guidelines may mean I'll lose some friends before I gain new ones. I want to honor You in this area, but sometimes, it is tough. It seems the girls that I attract are the ones who want to live for You, but quietly behind the scenes. Their fruit doesn't always align with what they say. I want friends who understand that God doesn't expect us to be perfect, but He does expect us to live a lifestyle pleasing to Him. Help me to center myself in You on days when I feel like nobody understands me. I even find myself sitting alone at lunch or hanging out in my dorm room alone because there are things I just refuse to do. I'm not perfect either, so if there's anything in me that may be pushing away a good friend, help me to see where I can improve. Forgive me for times I've chosen friends without running the person by You. This could've prevented some of the heartache I'm experiencing now. Please help me extend grace to myself in this area. This could also be a direct reflection of my growth in You. When we grow, things will fall off and fall away. I thank You that You're guiding me towards strong, sister relationships that will honor You. In the meantime, help me to draw closer to You and to relish in Your presence whenever I feel overwhelmed. I surrender this area of my life to You. Have Your way.

In Jesus name, Amen.

Reality Check

The truth about friendships often emerges when we hit college. People that we thought would always be there, end up falling away. People who we would've never chosen as friends, we end up seeing differently. Why is this? Because when we're younger, we usually choose off of popularity. Let's be honest. When we're in middle and high school, we're choosing girls based on how they look, dress and how fun their personality is. As we get older, we realize that those things just aren't enough. I have a lifetime friend that I wouldn't trade for anyone in the world, but that's very rare these days. We grew up together, so naturally, we always hung out. There have been seasons when we didn't talk, but God reconnected us in our thirties and we were able to pick up where we left off. If you have a friend that you've known all your life, don't cut them off just because you think the friendship is over. The whole point of this prayer is to ask God about all of your friendships. Hold them up to the Word and see if they align with His will for relationships. I went to an all-Girls' high school. Most of the girls who didn't want to hang with me, were popular, had lots of friends and always had a boyfriend.

I experienced this in middle school as well. But today, I can stand alone because of what those years of rejection taught me. I can also stand in a room full of people and draw great people to me. Instead of wallowing in the seasons where good friendships were hard to come by, I became the friend I wanted to be. Now, I understand the power of not giving everyone access to my oil, praying and asking God what value I'm supposed to add to someone's life in any given season, and how to navigate tough seasons where He wants me set apart. Sometimes, you have to be your own best friend before you can attract one. In the meantime, ask God to help you choose wisely and remember – the girl you admire may not be who God has for you and unpopular is usually purposeful.

<u>Scripture Meditation:</u>

Proverbs 27:9
The heartfelt counsel of a friend is as sweet as perfume and incense.

Proverbs 18:24
There are "friends" who destroy each other, but a real friend sticks closer than a brother.

Proverbs 27:6
Wounds from a sincere friend are better than many kisses from an enemy.

Proverbs 12:26
The godly give good advice to their friends; the wicked lead them astray.

Reflection Questions

1. What do you feel God is saying to you in this chapter?

____

____

____

____

2. Look at your friendship circle. Who do you need to ask God to remove and who should you keep?

____

____

____

____

3. Do you feel like a loner during this season of your life? If so, what could God be teaching you about friendships?

____

____

____

____

4. How can you use wisdom moving forward to choose Godly friendships that are pleasing to God?

____

____

____

____

SENIOR YEAR

Here's your third God Girl Challenge. Use your phone to open the video or download a QR reader from the App store.

16

Drowning in Studies

Dear God,

This has been a tough semester already. I find myself drowning in my studies and overwhelmed with everything on my plate. I know I haven't been making much time for You and I ask for Your forgiveness in this area. I barely have enough time just to be still and think. My mind is filled with so many words and formulas that I can't even think straight. But I know You sent me here to study what I'm studying, and You've given me the grace before to get through a semester. Maybe this time, I piled too many things on my plate. Help me to learn proper time management so that I can be successful. If there's anything on my plate that never should've been there, help me to figure out a way to remove it, even if it's a class. I know dropping a class may not always look good on paper, but if it's good for my mental health, help me to be obedient. Help me not to rush my four years. I think I let my ambition get the best of me and I tried to take on too much. Help me to realize that someone else's load doesn't have to be mine, so if I see my friend taking five classes a semester, that doesn't mean I have to. I pray for guidance and direction. Counsel me, Lord. Help me to take a step back and do what needs to be done. Now if You call for everything to remain the same, then that means You trust me with this load You've given me. I need to set aside time for You and put You back in Your rightful position in my life. Putting You first will allow for things in my life to run smoothly. Help me to trust You in this area. Give me strategy and wisdom to navigate this season with precision. If I make mistakes along the way, that's okay. You'll be right there to help me get through them. I thank You in advance for giving me supernatural strength to accomplish what I've set out to.

In Jesus name, Amen.

Reality Check

If God created the earth in six days, then sis, you can study for a test. But there are times where we've placed too much on our plates that God didn't tell us to take on. Perhaps you thought taking five classes, doing work study and joining a few organizations wouldn't be too much. One of the things that helped me not feel over-whelmed in college was remembering that I had four years. I think we tend to try to cram everything into the first year and then end up resenting college. I've seen people drop out because of this. College is naturally a bit stressful. Why add to that stress by taking on more than you have to? I took summer classes to balance out my four years. I didn't feel like I was giving anything up taking summer classes, either. I knew that I would be able to take four classes in the fall and still graduate on time. The only reason why I did an extra year was because I switched my major close to the fourth year. Please keep in mind that if God led you to this semester and you prayed about your classes and schedule, then He'll give you the grace and wisdom to get through. But you can't go to God in the beginning and then leave Him out of the process. Take Him with you. Pray daily and find scriptures to speak over your semester. When you get overwhelmed, that's not a means to quit. Overwhelm is usually a sign that you're trying to do things in your own strength. Rest, but don't quit. Resting could mean taking a break from studying and going to do something fun. It could literally be lying down and closing your eyes for an hour. When God sees that you're being responsible and handling your business, He'll give you the grace to take the breaks you need without missing a beat.

<u>Scripture Meditation:</u>

Philippians 4:8
And now, dear brothers and sisters, one final thing. Fix your thoughts on what is true, and honorable, and right, and pure, and lovely, and admirable. Think about things that are excellent and worthy of praise.

Psalm 94:19
When doubts filled my mind, your comfort gave me renewed hope and cheer.

Jeremiah 17:7-8
"But blessed are those who trust in the Lord
and have made the Lord their hope and confidence.
They are like trees planted along a riverbank,
with roots that reach deep into the water.
Such trees are not bothered by the heat
or worried by long months of drought.
Their leaves stay green,
and they never stop producing fruit."

Matthew 11:28-30

Then Jesus said, "Come to me, all of you who are weary and carry heavy burdens, and I will give you rest. Take my yoke upon you. Let me teach you, because I am humble and gentle at heart, and you will find rest for your souls. For my yoke is easy to bear, and the burden I give you is light."

Reflection Questions

1. What do you feel God is saying to you in this chapter?

____

____

____

____

2. How do you take a break when you need one?

____

____

____

____

3. Two of the things I wish I knew about in college are self-care and soul care. Ask God to give you a remedy for both and write it down. Spend some quiet time with Him to discover what this looks like for you.

____

____

____

____

4. Ask God to show you where you may have things on your plate that He never told you to take on. This could be school responsibilities or even personal ones.

____

____

____

____

17

❦

Social Disaster

Dear God,

Lord, I know that I've been scrolling more than I've been reading the Word. I've been posting more than I've been praying. I don't want to become a social disaster. Someone who is only social online but can't have conversations in real life. I also don't want to succumb to the pressures of social media. Help me to put boundaries in place when it comes to social media. If this means taking it off my phone (and not going on the browser), give me the discipline to do so. If it's just a matter of placing limitations on my screen time, help me to do so. Whatever it takes to not become addicted to something that could cause me mental health issues and that could disconnect me from reality, do it. I know that I can't just ask You to do it. I have to help You help me. Give me the discipline and fortitude to back away from social media for as long as I need to. Teach me how to do social media Your way when I am on there. Keep my mind stayed on You so that I can stay in perfect peace. Help me not to take on other's thoughts and ideologies because I'm scrolling too much. Keep me from being inundated with ideas and beliefs that contradict what Your word says. I pray for clarity as You walk me through who to unfollow on my social media accounts. Sometimes, we're following people and businesses that compromise their integrity or show compromising things and we think nothing of it. I don't want to become so oblivious that I disregard the way You would feel about things. Lord, take over my social media. Help me to start from scratch if I have to. If I'm struggling with comparison, help me to see that this could be the reason why. Help me to guard my heart and my mind.

In Jesus name, Amen.

<u>Reality Check</u>

There's no secret that being on social media too much can cause depression. But before it even gets to depression, what is it costing us spiritually? One of the things I don't ever want us as believers to get too comfortable with is thinking of all the reasons why something isn't good for us, but not thinking of how it affects us spiritually. Putting God first in this area means remembering that your social media belongs to God. You're a representation of Him and what you believe. People should go to your pages and see nothing less than a representation of Christ. This is why I always say, "God in my bio really is God in my life." Some people may try to separate their social media from God, but how is that even possible? In addition to that, spending a lot of time on social media can cause you to start taking on ideologies and beliefs that God never intended for you to take on. Before you ask if it's that deep, it is. Images can literally stay in our minds for days and weeks after seeing them. Are you being mindful of who you follow? Are you just hitting the follow button on every celebrity that has a page or are you making sure that they aren't showing too much skin before you follow? Our eyes are literally the window to our souls. In the prayer on entertainment choices, I talk about this. Social media has actually become another form of television. The difference is, it's bite-sized entertainment, and we can absorb it quicker. Most people on social media are a social disaster, meaning they can function well online, but they can't even hold a conversation with someone in real time, in real life. Don't become that person. God intends for us to have real, meaningful community with people. Not with images and videos. If you've never done one, I encourage you to do a social media fast for at least a month. Start with seven days, then work your way up. I guarantee you, you won't miss a thing. Then, when you're ready to come back ask God to help you clean up your social media by following positive accounts (they don't all have to be Christian), unfollowing any accounts that He tells you to and being mindful of what you post and like. Remember, whatever you like, you agree with.

<u>Scripture Meditation:</u>

Psalm 1:1
Oh, the joys of those who do not
follow the advice of the wicked,
or stand around with sinners,
or join in with mockers.

2 Timothy 2:23
Again I say, don't get involved in foolish, ignorant arguments that only start fights.

Psalm 41:6
They visit me as if they were my friends,

but all the while they gather gossip,
and when they leave, they spread it everywhere.

Proverbs 23:25-27
Look straight ahead,
and fix your eyes on what lies before you.
Mark out a straight path for your feet;
stay on the safe path.
Don't get sidetracked;
keep your feet from following evil.

<u>*Reflection Questions*</u>

1. What do you feel God is saying to you in this chapter?

____

____

____

____

2. How much time do you spend on social media daily? Check your screen time on your phone if you have an iPhone. If you don't, guess.

____

____

____

____

3. What pages do you follow that you know you shouldn't? For example, as much as I love Cardi B's personality, I do not follow her on social. Clean up your social during this time.

____

____

____

____

4. How can you dedicate your social media to God? For example, I'm not going to like something that I know clearly speaks against God's word and I'm not going to follow someone who displays sinful behavior on their page.

____

____

____

____

18

Fasting Feature

Dear God,

Lord, I feel led to fast. I've never really done this before, but I know that I've seen my church family participate in fasting. I know that it's a spiritual practice that can truly help me tap deeper into who You are. I have a big decision in front of me and I need Your guidance. I also feel spiritual apathy coming on and I don't want to become complacent in my walk. I'm praying that You lead me into the fast that's best for me in this season. It could be a digital/technology fast or a complete food fast – whichever one You lead me to do, help me to stick to what I agree to. Even with this being my first time, this fast can still be successful. I pray that You would lead me to scriptures and sermons during this time of fasting that speak to where I'm at. I want to draw closer to You and come out of this fast refreshed, with clarity and wisdom. Help me to realize that this fast isn't about getting You to do what I want You to do – it's about starving my flesh and feeding my spirit. It's about drawing closer to the Holy Spirit so that I can be led into all truth. The enemy is deceptive, and I don't want to be caught off guard by his tactics. I want to break any stronghold that may be on my life and I know fasting will help me to do that. Give me the fortitude, strength and desire to fast. Help me to step back to obtain the clarity I need. Not just for this decision I need to make, but also to know how to navigate my daily life. The Holy Spirit is here with me minute-by-minute and I can call on Him whenever I'm in need. Help me to realize that after this fast is over, I can create a rhythm of fasting by setting aside time each week to draw closer to You.

In Jesus name, Amen.

Reality Check

Fasting has become one of my favorite things to do. I know that sounds so weird for a foodie like me, but the truth is, taking a step away from the chaos of the world and truly getting re-centered in Christ could mean more than just reading some scriptures and throwing on some worship music. You have to dig deep in order to really get to the different places God wants you to go in Him. I started fasting once a week almost four years ago. Of course, throughout the years I've missed a few weeks, but I try to fast at least two to three times a month. There's something about spending a full day with God with no interruptions that just brings me joy. Now, if I'm honest, I'm still growing in this area. There will be times I say I'm going to do a full day of no television, social media and fast from food from 6am to 6pm. This means, my intention is to eat after 6pm, but keep myself from electronics for the entire day. I still find myself hopping on Instagram after 6pm and watching a movie around 8pm. It is hard, but I'm still working on it. I shared that to encourage you not to see your fast as a failure if you eat a cracker at noon because you either forgot you were fasting or you felt famished. God intends for us to keep our word to Him, no doubt, but He's more concerned with your heart posture and you drawing closer to Him than a list of rules. This is why I advise you to start off slowly. Try fasting from sunrise until noon before you jump into a whole day. Try fasting from one meal instead of all three. Try eliminating social media and electronics for half a day before trying a week. The best thing to do is to ask God what type of fast He wants you to do, then stick to it. Grab an accountability partner your first couple of times fasting. This can help you as you'll have somebody to check in with throughout the fast. I encourage you to make this a part of your lifestyle. Trust me, you'll be amazed at the results.

<u>*Scripture Meditation:*</u>

Isaiah 58:6-9
"No, this is the kind of fasting I want:
Free those who are wrongly imprisoned;
  lighten the burden of those who work for you.
Let the oppressed go free,
  and remove the chains that bind people.
Share your food with the hungry,
  and give shelter to the homeless.
Give clothes to those who need them,
  and do not hide from relatives who need your help.
  "Then your salvation will come like the dawn,
  and your wounds will quickly heal.
Your godliness will lead you forward,
  and the glory of the Lord will protect you from behind.
Then when you call, the Lord will answer.
  'Yes, I am here,' he will quickly reply.

Daniel 9:3-5

So I turned to the Lord God and pleaded with him in prayer and fasting. I also wore rough burlap and sprinkled myself with ashes. I prayed to the Lord my God and confessed: "O Lord, you are a great and awesome God! You always fulfill your covenant and keep your promises of unfailing love to those who love you and obey your commands. But we have sinned and done wrong. We have rebelled against you and scorned your commands and regulations.

Joel 2:12

That is why the Lord says, "Turn to me now, while there is time. Give me your hearts. Come with fasting, weeping, and mourning.

Reflection Questions

1. What do you feel God is saying to you in this chapter?

____

____

____

____

2. Have you ever fasted before? If not, list the reasons why. If so, how can you strengthen your fasting?

____

____

____

____

3. As you meditate on these verses, what are some ways you may have used fasting incorrectly in the past? If you've never fasted, list some preconceived notions you had about fasting (i.e. I thought fasting was to get what you wanted from God, etc.).

____

____

____

____

4. Now that you have a better understanding of fasting, how can you incorporate it into your spiritual walk on a regular basis?

____

____

____

____

19

Mental Madness

Dear God,

Father, I need You bad. I feel like I'm spiraling, and I can't seem to catch my breath. I've heard people talking about depression and anxiety, but up until now, I'd never really experienced it. I don't know what to do, but I know the first step is calling on You. Help me to find my grip and to hold onto Your hand as You send in reinforcements. Right now, I need prayer warriors to lift me up in prayer and to war for me, because I don't have the strength to war for myself. Show me who I can trust with this pain. Help me not to turn to negative or dark outlets to overcome this, but to know that there are resources out there that can assist me. I speak against the spirit of suicide and depression and command them to bow in Your presence. I decree and declare peace according to Philippians 4:6-7. I access Your peace right now. I decree joy where there was sorrow. I know this prayer is just a seed and that I may have to seek a thera-pist, but for now, Lord, I just need You to reach down and grab me.

Help me find my footing again so that I can take the steps necessary to get the help I need. Reveal to me what brought me to this place. If it was anything that I allowed into my space, help me to remove it. Sometimes, depression can be triggered by negative relationships and I don't want to be naïve to that fact. I plead the blood of Jesus over my mind and I decree that with my mind, I serve You. I have the mind of Christ. I take every thought captive and submit it to the obedience of Jesus Christ. I will not give up and I will not allow my circumstances to drown me. I trust You to guide me through this season and lead me safely to the other side of the storm.

In Jesus name, Amen.

Reality Check

I suffered from deep depression, anxiety/panic attacks and paranoia in college. It was so bad that during my junior year I begged my mom to 302 me. If you're not sure what that means, it's basically asking to be committed to a psych ward so that you can get psychiatric help. I have never officially been diagnosed with anything, but I always say that it doesn't take a genius to see if you have some mental instability. I learned in my late twenties, that my family actually battles heavily with depression on both sides. It is possible to have seasons of depression just because life gets hard and times can be turbulent, but there are some people who suffer from chronic depression and most times, it is genetic. It sucks, because I always say if our parents and grandparents had done their part to kill some of the stuff that's damaging our bloodlines, then I wouldn't have had to fight it. But the reality is, God chooses a David and Joseph for every bloodline. It's not our job to point the finger, we just have to rise up and kill what's trying to kill us. Since you're in college please know that you have access to free counselors. There are licensed professionals that you have access to. Don't let this resource pass you by.

I wish I had taken advantage of this when I was in undergrad, but I didn't. Now, I have to pay for therapy (LOL), which is fine, but the reality is, your trauma and pain will cost you. It will either cost you mentally, emotionally and maybe even physically, or it will cost you financially. I think the latter is better. Get the help and assistance you need before it's too late. And contrary to church culture's belief – you can have Jesus and therapy. Going to therapy doesn't mean you've left Jesus out of the equation and having Jesus doesn't mean you don't need therapy. As my girl Dr. Anita Phillips always says, "prayer is a weapon, therapy is a strategy". God cares about your mental and emotional health just as much as He does your spiritual health. Ask God for a strategy to help you with your mental health and disregard the naysayers, even if it's your own voice of fear.

Scripture Meditation:

Isaiah 41:10
Don't be afraid, for I am with you.
Don't be discouraged, for I am your God.
I will strengthen you and help you.
I will hold you up with my victorious right hand.

1 Peter 5:7-8
Give all your worries and cares to God, for he cares about you. Stay alert! Watch out for your great enemy, the devil. He prowls around like a roaring lion, looking for someone to devour.

2 Corinthians 10:5
We destroy every proud obstacle that keeps people from knowing God. We capture their rebellious thoughts and teach them to obey Christ.

1 Peter 5:10

In his kindness God called you to share in his eternal glory by means of Christ Jesus. So after you have suffered a little while, he will restore, support, and strengthen you, and he will place you on a firm foundation.

Reflection Questions

1. What do you feel God is saying to you in this chapter?

____

____

____

____

2. Did you grow up in a family that was against therapy as a Christian? If so, write how that has affected your views on going to therapy.

____

____

____

____

3. Have you considered therapy before or are you currently going to therapy? If so, write how you believe (or how it has) helped you in your walk with Christ.

____

____

____

____

4. Study Paul. Take some time and read the new testament. Write five ways you realize that Paul was suffering from depression and anxiety. Then write five ways you see Paul in your own life.

____

____

____

____

20

Family Balance

Dear God,

Father, I just had an argument with my parents. They feel like I've completely forgotten them since I got to school. I feel like they aren't letting me breathe or grow up. I know it's important to prioritize my family, but sometimes I feel like they smother me and haven't even allowed me to enjoy my independence. I'm asking You to step into this situation and help all of us see where we can improve. Maybe I should go home a little more so that I can spend time with them, but I also need them to let me build my life the way I want. Keep me humble so that I don't think I don't need my parents or just because I'm out of the house, I can be disrespectful. But I feel pressured. I feel like my family doesn't get that I moved away to get away from some of the drama and control. I want to honor my parents, but I also want to have some freedom. Show me Lord where I can do better and how I can fix this. If I need to take my hands off the situation and allow You to fix it, show me how to do that. In the meantime, help me smooth things over with my parents because I don't like that we both said things that were hurtful. I submit my tongue and words to You and ask that You help me to have a healthy conversation with my parents once You give me the green light. Forgive me for any wrong I've done and moving forward, show me how to express my needs without getting frustrated. I know You'll guide us to a reasonable solution.

In Jesus Name, Amen.

<u>*Reality Check*</u>

I think a lot of parents struggle with this because they give so much to their children as they're growing up and if they're honest, they feel like their child owes them something. I also believe that parents who made their lives all about their children end up not knowing what to do once their children leave the nest. This can be detrimental to the relationship as the child nears adulthood. My mom and I have always been close. She is my best friend. But if I'm honest, once I turned eighteen, I wanted the freedom she never really allowed me to have when I was growing up. My mother didn't really smother me, but I was raised in a strict, Christian household, so a lot of things that I wanted to do, I didn't get to do. Some of them, I probably didn't need to do, but for the most part, I was just a teenager who wanted to enjoy her teen years. My worst behavior was talking too much in class, so I wasn't looking for any trouble. My mother and I struggled a lot during my college years because I wanted to live my own life. I rebelled, like most children end up doing. Only I was rebelling in my adult years and that didn't make sense to me. In many ways, my approach was wrong, and I could've handled things better. But she also had to recognize her mistakes. She had to learn to let go and while it was difficult, today, I have my own ministry, a business and several published books. That means that she did her part. When it comes to you being away at school and feeling like your parents aren't letting you grow up, remember this: you too, have to learn how to be a good daughter. You can't call home when you need money but not check in to see how they're doing. Your parents love you and they just want to know that they haven't lost you. If you're struggling in this area, ask God to show you how you can meet your parents halfway. This could be going home one weekend and cooking dinner for them. Then the next weekend, you hang with your friends on campus. Tell them how you feel. I also think cards and letters help in this situation. Writing them and sending them love notes can show them that you haven't forgotten them and that you appreciate them. Family is needed and you don't want to look up and realize that you've missed very important times with your family all because you wanted to be so independent. Cherish the times you have with them as much as you can. I have friends who've lost both of their parents and they wish they could turn back the hands of time. Ask God to help you find balance so that everyone's needs can be met with Him being at the center of those needs.

Scripture Meditation:

Exodus 20:12
"Honor your father and mother. Then you will live a long, full life in the land the Lord your God is giving you."

Colossians 3:13
Make allowance for each other's faults, and forgive anyone who offends you. Remember, the Lord forgave you, so you must forgive others.

Ephesians 6:1-4

Children, obey your parents because you belong to the Lord, for this is the right thing to do. "Honor your father and mother." This is the first commandment with a promise: If you honor your father and mother, "things will go well for you, and you will have a long life on the earth. Fathers, do not provoke your children to anger by the way you treat them. Rather, bring them up with the discipline and instruction that comes from the Lord.

Reflection Questions

1. What do you feel God is saying to you in this chapter?

____

____

____

____

2. Have you been dishonoring your parents lately? List any ways that you've dishonored your parents (based on the word of God, not their personal desires for you). If not, list the things you do to make sure you stay obedient in this area.

____

____

____

____

3. How can you strengthen your relationship with your parents?

____

____

____

____

4. Do you feel that your parents won't let you grow up? If so, write a letter to them asking them to trust you more, but also highlighting how they may be trying to take over God's role in your life. Pray about this first. If this question doesn't apply to you, write a letter to your parents thanking them for trusting you and raising you in Christ.

21

Dream Chasers

Dear God,

Father, I want to be focused on You more than I am the dream I'm chasing. Help me not to lose focus on what really matters. I don't want to get the dream job or dream life and forget about You. The best way for me to not do that is to put You first and to not get caught up in the rat race. I see it on social media, on campus and even in my own family. I know that dreams are important to You and that You place desires in our heart so that we can know what to pursue. But in my pursuit of those desires, help me to make You my first pursuit. I love that You're trusting me with this dream, but I also know that it won't be all peaches and cream. There will be challenges and there will be resistance, so help me to focus on building my character more than I build my dream. Building my character will help me be able to sustain the dream when I get there. I do get weary and lonely sometimes, because dream chasers usually have visions that many people don't understand, but You'll supply me with the tribe I need in due season. In the meantime, give me the grace and peace to stand on the dream You've given me. Help me to maximize my time by learning about the field You've assigned me to. I trust You to continue to unfold the dream according to Your perfect will for my life. Help me not to get ahead of You or to try to manipulate the process. If You've shown me people I'll work with or places I'll go, help me to trust that You'll bring me into that in Your timing. I don't want to jump ahead of the process that You've placed me in. The valley is just as important as the mountaintop. Help me not to rush to the top, but to enjoy the climb. I trust You with my dreams.

In Jesus name, Amen.

<u>Reality Check</u>

When I graduated from Temple, I remember feeling depressed. I couldn't believe that I'd been sending out resumes since junior year, yet I had nothing to show for it. No jobs in my field in sight. I didn't know what I'd done wrong for it to end up like this. I was devastated. I was still working my security job when I graduated, and it was so confusing to me. I took a year off, then went to graduate school. I was struggling financially and felt like such a failure. That's when I started to really study Joseph. My mom would mention how I was a lot like Joseph throughout the years, so I decided to tap into his story. Today, I can relate more to Joseph than ever before. Here's the truth: If God shows you a dream for your life and places specific desires in your heart, your job is to trust the steps He orders you to take and leave the results up to Him. That can be hard when you feel like you have the skills and talents to succeed. When I look back over my journey, I actually thank God that He didn't open some of the doors I wanted Him to open. Why? Because I had a horrible anger problem and was emotionally immature in my twenties. Can you imagine if He had opened that door for me to work at Essence magazine at that time? I would've destroyed my reputation. If He would've opened the doors to the big offices in New York where someone mentioning your name in a negative way one time could destroy you for years to come, I would've hit rock bottom. One thing I love about Joseph is that he didn't chase the dream. He was led by God. There will be pitfalls, obstacles and resistance on your journey, whether you're chasing a dream or not. But for those of us who God has given large visions to, the path will be harder. Today, I can stand with integrity and a level of emotional maturity that I never thought I would achieve. Because I let God do what He needed to do internally, I don't have to worry about destroying things externally. I've developed more patience than I ever thought I would have. In the last four years, I've pitched two TV ideas to major studios or companies in Hollywood; I've written for a magazine and had a celebrity cover story; I've written and published fifteen books (including this one); I've run several businesses and I've started a ministry. God didn't allow me to experience all of that because I deserve it. It's because His word is true, and His plan is still unfolding. I'm still waiting for the fullness of the dream to manifest, but God has allowed me to experience it in bite-sized pieces. If there's one thing I want you to take away from this chapter, it's this: Your dream's GPS is God's power and Spirit. Without them, you'll always be headed in the wrong direction. Sometimes, God will lead you the long way to get to your dreams because He knows that some of those pit stops are required for you to become the best version of yourself. Lean in and enjoy the ride.

Scripture Meditation:

Psalm 143:10
Teach me to do your will, for you are my God. May your gracious Spirit lead me forward on a firm footing.

Psalm 33:11
But the Lord's plans stand firm forever; his intentions can never be shaken.

Psalm 37:4-5
Take delight in the Lord, and he will give you your heart's desires. Commit everything you do to the Lord. Trust him, and he will help you.

Ecclesiastes 11:6
Plant your seed in the morning and keep busy all afternoon, for you don't know if profit will come from one activity or another—or maybe both.

Reflection Questions

1. What do you feel God is saying to you in this chapter?

\
\
\
\

2. How can you chase God more than you chase your dreams? What steps can you implement to stay on track?

\
\
\
\

3. Do you feel that you're chasing a God-given dream? If not, ask God to show you what your God-given dream is and write it down.

\
\
\
\

4. How can you better serve God with your dreams and desires?

\
\
\
\

Permission to Fail

Bonus Prayer #1

Dear God,

Father, help me to not be so hard on myself when it looks like I've failed. Help me to give myself permission to fail. I know that in today's culture, that isn't the norm, but if I give myself permission to fail, then I'm giving myself permission to access Your grace on another level. I thank You for the things You've placed in front of me to work on, build or grow, but help me to realize that since the outcome is in Your hands, I don't have to stress over whether or not it will work out. Failing isn't the end and You can bring treasure out of failure. I give You permission to take me along a journey of failure if it brings me closer to You. Again, this isn't a normal prayer to pray, but so many people in my generation are chasing success and prosperity, not realizing that failure is where their growth happens. Failure is where you find out what you're made of. Help me to see failure from Your perspective. I don't have to broadcast my failures for them to be seen as authentic, but I can bring them to You and ask You to show me how You will still use this for Your glory. Failure can be optimized in Your hands. I thank You for helping me to extend grace to myself during seasons where failure seems to be all I see. Praying this prayer helps me to see things in a healthier way. I won't feel so pressured to make everything succeed by my own hands, or to hit the mark 100% of the time. Maybe that last semester was supposed to go that way or that business was supposed to fail because You knew that I wasn't ready to handle the magnitude of success that I desire. Help me to learn from my mistakes and failures and to trust You to turn them into treasured gold.

In Jesus Name, Amen.

<u>*Reality Check*</u>

One of the things that I fear for the generation behind me is that so many of you are afraid to fail. I see it up and down your timelines, in your language and in your pursuits. If you don't hit the bullseye every time, you end up wanting to throw in the towel altogether. I wish that someone had taught us more about grace when I was growing up, but what I'm praying that you get from this chapter is that grace isn't just for when you sin. It's for your entire life. God doesn't see failure as the end. He sees it as a new beginning. He can take any failure and turn it into a new beginning if You trust Him with it, but You have to be okay with failing. I love that Generation Z takes big risks and that you guys are so innovative and ambitious. You can build a business in three months and kill it. But you can also be easily offended and can become desensitized to reality a lot easier than back in my day. Because of this, I often feel that you've perceived success and failure in the wrong way. You look at success as your bottom line and failure as the end of life. This is why the suicide rate is so high among Gen Z. It saddens me because the harder you are on yourself, the more the enemy tries to plant seeds in your mind to bring about your destruction. I told you how I felt after I graduated from college. I just thank God that by the time I graduated, the depression and anxiety attacks were under control. If they weren't, I would've probably ended up in a downward spiral myself. As I learn more and more about grace, what I realize is that God intends for us to access His grace second by second, not just when we do something wrong. He wants us to step into His grace in every area of our lives. He also wants us to not only extend grace to others, but to ourselves. Take failure as an opportunity to learn more and to see how your character was developed in the process. I promise you – God can turn that failure into a win if you stick it out.

Scripture Meditation:

Jeremiah 8:4

"Jeremiah, say to the people, 'This is what the Lord says: When people fall down, don't they get up again? When they discover they're on the wrong road, don't they turn back?"

Proverbs 24:16

The godly may trip seven times, but they will get up again.
But one disaster is enough to overthrow the wicked.

2 Corinthians 4:9

We are hunted down, but never abandoned by God. We get knocked down, but we are not destroyed.

Psalm 40:2-3

He lifted me out of the pit of despair,

out of the mud and the mire.
He set my feet on solid ground
    and steadied me as I walked along.
He has given me a new song to sing,
    a hymn of praise to our God.
Many will see what he has done and be amazed.
    They will put their trust in the Lord.

<u>*Reflection Questions*</u>

1. What do you feel God is saying to you in this chapter?

____

____

____

____

2. Name a time you failed and instead of taking that failure to God, you beat yourself up.

____

____

____

____

3. Write out three ways you now see failure as something God can use for His good.

____

____

____

____

4. Write out some steps you will take the next time failure is staring you in the face. How will you overcome it?

____

____

____

____

23

Daddy's Girl

Bonus Prayer #2

Dear God,

Sometimes it's hard seeing my friends getting visits from their fathers on campus. I see them with this earthly love that I have missed out on. As a young woman, I thought by now that my father and I would have a more solid relationship, but we don't. If I'm honest, I'm tired of trying. He's the father and he should be reaching for me. I have forgiven him and tried to build a relationship with him, yet he seems to be too busy to even take a minute to see me. I'm coming to You asking for Your guidance and healing in this area. I choose to honor my father, although he may not be treating me fairly right now. I want to have a pure heart and not an unforgiving heart, so I thank You right now for changing my heart posture. Help me to see how his absence was a part of Your divine protection for me when I was younger. He may not have been equipped to give me the things that I needed. While that may have been hard for me to understand then, I am working to understand this now. Help me to know that You're a Father to the fatherless and you set the solitary in families. Thank You that my mother was everything that I needed in a parent and where she couldn't, You made up the difference. I thank You for showing me more of You in this situation. The times I've wanted to run to my father, I've run to You. I know that You've never missed a recital or a special moment in my life. I pray healing over my father's heart and that You will reveal to him the error in his ways while also showing him Your love and grace. Mend my broken heart and keep me focused on You.

In Jesus Name, Amen.

Reality Check

Let me just tell you right now – this was not the prayer I prayed for my father when I was in college. I was too filled with bitterness and resentment to utter these words. It wasn't until a few years ago where I even had the capacity to understand that my forgiveness for my father couldn't be conditional. I used to say things like, "I'll forgive him, but hopefully, he'll call more," or "I forgive him, but I don't need to talk to him". Essentially, God opened my eyes to see that real forgiveness is forgiving without adding a condition. While there was nothing wrong with wanting my father to call more, there was something wrong with taking my forgiveness back just because he didn't. I may have never said that I was taking my forgiveness back, but the heart speaks even when the mouth doesn't. For any young woman dealing with an absent father, please know that God sees you. It wasn't and will never be your fault. Even if your mother played a role in your father staying away, he could've fought harder for you and done his best to do right by you. I pray that you will open your heart to God and ask Him to shine a light into your heart to expel out any darkness that may be hiding. Sometimes, we verbally forgive someone, but there's some leftover residue still in the crevices of our hearts. Resentment and bitterness can block clarity and progress. You want your college years to be full of freedom, so it's important to do constant heart checks. Don't be afraid to vent to God about your frustrations regarding your father, but also ask Him to love on you so much that you don't have room to hate him. This isn't easy and will require that you constantly spend time in God's presence. It will also require your complete vulnerability with God to be able to acknowledge that this still hurts you. Trust me, it gets better with time. This doesn't mean that you'll be completely over it, especially if you've opened the door for your father to be a part of your life but he continues to let you down; however, it does allow for you to have a clear heart knowing you've done your part.

<u>Scripture Meditation</u>

Psalm 68:5-6
Father to the fatherless, defender of widows—
this is God, whose dwelling is holy.
God places the lonely in families;
he sets the prisoners free and gives them joy.
But he makes the rebellious live in a sun-scorched land.

Psalm 27:10
Even if my father and mother abandon me,
the Lord will hold me close.

Romans 8:15-17
So you have not received a spirit that makes you fearful slaves. Instead, you received God's Spirit when he adopted you as his own children. Now we call him, "Abba, Father." For his Spirit joins with

our spirit to affirm that we are God's children. And since we are his children, we are his heirs. In fact, together with Christ we are heirs of God's glory. But if we are to share his glory, we must also share his suffering.

Psalm 127:3-4
Children are a gift from the Lord;
they are a reward from him.
Children born to a young man
are like arrows in a warrior's hands.

Reflection Questions

1. What do you feel God is saying to you in this chapter?

____

____

____

____

2. If you struggle in your relationship with your father, how do you feel after reading this chapter? If you don't, what challenges do you find in your relationship with your father that distort your view of God?

____

____

____

____

3. Ask God to highlight any unforgiveness in your heart toward your father. Even if he is in your life, there are certainly times that he's let you down. Write your responses below.

____

____

____

____

4. If you could write a letter to your father, whether he's absent, in prison, or at home right now, what would you say?

____

____

____

FINAL CHALLENGE

Here's your final God Girl Challenge. Use your phone to open the video or download a QR reader from the App store.

24

Resource Guide

The list below is full of music, television shows and movies that are suitable for a Christian to indulge in. Even with this list, you should be mindful not to binge too much or place these things above your relationship with God, but they are meant to help guide you into safer ways to live a pleasing life to Him while you are here on earth.

<u>*Music*</u>

Pursuit of, Love. By Uninvtd & SAINT (album)
No Stranger by Natalie Grant (album)
Kierra Sheard
Tauren Wells
Maverick City
Switch
Tribl
Zoe Music

Da'TRUTH
Lecrae
Canton Jones
Lauren Diagle
Koryn Hawthorne
Naomi Raine
One House Worship
Tim Bowman, Jr.
Travis Greene
Will Reagan & United Pursuit

Secular artists who have clean music (some of these artists are also Christians)
Alessia Cara
Tori Kelly
Esperanza Spalding
Carrie Underwood
Lady A (formally Lady Antebellum)
Emeli Sande
Lalah Hathaway
Leona Lewis

<u>Television Shows</u>

All American
A Million Little Things
Chicago P.D.
Chicago Med
9-1-1
The Good Doctor
Shark Tank

Old Shows in Syndication/Streaming (Netflix or Hulu)
Family Matters
Moesha
Hangin' with Mr. Cooper
Parenthood
Sister, Sister
My Wife & Kids
CSI: Miami
This Is Us
Switched at Birth
Friday Night Lights (this is a movie also)

<u>*Movies*</u>
Step Up
Just Wright
The Upside
The United States Vs. Billie Holiday
Beethoven (all of them)
What A Girl Wants
Domestic Disturbance
Hitch
Once I Was A Beehive
Greater
The Blindside

Mya Kay
Photo Credit: Ardell McDuffie

Born and raised in North Philadelphia, Mya K. Douglas, professionally known as Mya Kay, is an Amazon bestselling author, speaker and literary consultant. She has written and co-written several books, including, *The Clover Chronicles* series and *Before Empire: Raising Bryshere "Yazz the Greatest" Gray*. She owns Girls Anthem, a full-service literary consulting firm that equips women with the tools they need to write their stories and build successful writing careers. Mya is also the creator and host of "The Mya Kay Show", a literary podcast that features writing tips, exclusive interviews and publishing success stories. You can learn more about her at www.writermya.com and www.girlsanthem.biz.

www.ingramcontent.com/pod-product-compliance
Lightning Source LLC
Chambersburg PA
CBHW031302060726
47590CB00003B/1024